Seeds of a Nation

Indiana

P. M. Boekhoff and Stuart A. Kallen

KidHaven Press, an imprint of Gale Group, Inc.

P.O. Box 289009, San Diego, CA 92198-9009

On cover: *The Battle of Tippecanoe*

Library of Congress Cataloging-in-Publication Data

Boekhoff, P. M. (Patti Marlene), 1957–
    Indiana/by P. M. Boekhoff and Stuart A. Kallen.
        p. cm.—(Seeds of a Nation)
    Includes bibliographical references and index.
    Summary: Discusses the history of Indiana, its Native Americans,
    changes caused by the arrival of the British and the French, the devasta-
    tion of the Indian tribes, and statehood.
    ISBN 0-7377-0663-5 (alk. paper)
    1. Indiana—Juvenile literature. [1. Indiana.] I. Kallen, Stuart A.,
1955–   . II. Title. III. Seeds of a Nation (Series)
    F526.3 .B64 2002
    977.2—dc21   00-012812

Contents

Chapter One

"Indian Land"

Indiana is the thirty-eighth largest state in the United States. It is located in the Midwest region between Lake Michigan and the Ohio River and between the states of Illinois and Ohio. The name Indiana means "Indian Land," and the Native Americans, called "Indians" by the European explorers, were the first settlers in the area. Indiana has been a crossroads of trade since Native Americans lived there. Today the motto of Indiana is "The Crossroads of America."

The First People

About three thousand years ago, early Native Americans built cities along the Ohio River, out of large mounds of earth from the riverbed and wood from the forest. The Mound Builders were farmers who traded with other tribes on the many trails that crossed through the Indiana settlements. Angel Mounds, near

Evansville, is the largest mound city in Indiana. It includes earth houses, public buildings, temples, burial mounds, and forts. Thousands of people lived at Angel Mounds from A.D. 1100 to 1450.

The Mound Builders grew corn, beans, squash, melons, pumpkins, sunflowers, and other plants in the fertile river valley. They preserved and stored these foods for winter, along with dried herbs and berries. They also grew tobacco, which they considered a sacred herb. Tobacco was smoked at religious ceremonies in pipes carved from soft pipestone.

INDIANA'S PLACE IN THE UNITED STATES TODAY

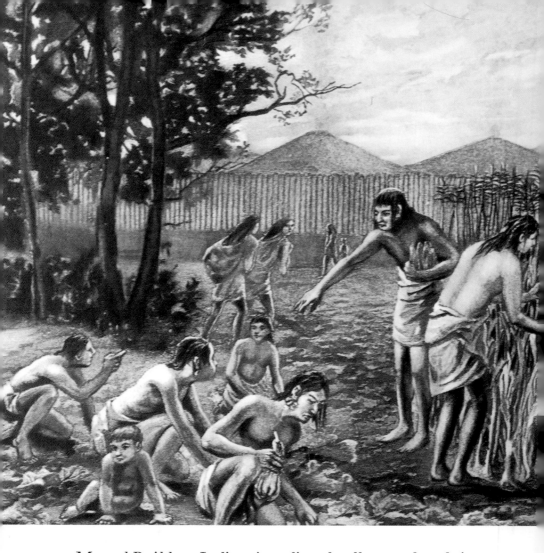

Mound Builders, Indiana's earliest dwellers, gather their crops.

Between 1450 and 1600, the ancient cultures along the Ohio River mysteriously disappeared. Soon other tribes moved into the region, such as the Miami, Shawnee, Delaware, and Potawatomi. Members of these tribes were probably distant relatives of the Mound Builders. They came from as far away as the East Coast and began to farm the land along the rivers. All of these tribes spoke related languages known as Algonquian.

The Miami

By the 1600s the main residents of Indiana were the Miami tribe, who called themselves Twightwee (Twat-wa). This name makes a sound similar to the cry of cranes, which could be heard along the waterways. Like the Mound Builders before them, the Miami farmed the fertile soil of the river valleys. They also fished and hunted along the waterways. To travel on the water, they built boats called dugout canoes. Each canoe was made from a single tree, usually a butternut, that was hollowed out and carved with beautiful geometic and animal designs.

The Miami also decorated their shirts, leggings, dresses, and moccasins that were made from white-tailed deerskins. These items were colorfully acorned with embroidery as well as paint, shells, and feathers, which were also made into jewelry.

Though everyone helped with the work, women made most of the clothing and tepees for their families, and men built most of the large buildings. The Miami lived in longhouses, rectangular buildings about 25 feet wide and up to 150 feet long. These large homes were built with logs, then covered with elm bark or mats woven of rushes. Up to seven families lived in each longhouse. Each village also had a large public building that was used for councils and ceremonies.

The Buffalo Hunt

Daily life in a Miami village changed with the seasons. In the fall, after the crops were harvested, men, women,

Hunting buffalo became easier after Europeans brought horses to the region.

and children packed up their belongings and traveled to the nearby prairie to hunt buffalo. For this reason, the Miami are sometimes called Prairie Algonquians.

Hunting buffalo was a difficult task before the Europeans brought horses and guns to the region in the 1600s. Hunters had to stalk their prey on foot, then trap and confuse the buffalo. To capture their prey, Miami hunters built a large ring of fire, open at one end. The hunters **stampeded** the buffalo, yelling and shouting to guide them into the ring of fire. The frightened buffalo were then shot with arrows.

After a successful hunt, women and children prepared the buffalo hides and meat to take back home to the river valley. Every part of the buffalo was used. Meat was eaten, hides were used for robes and sleeping mats, and bones were made into tools and sewing needles.

Ceremonies and Celebrations

Although the Miami hunted buffalo, they also believed the animals were sacred and they silently offered an apology and a prayer for them before they were killed. In addition to buffalo, the Miami believed that everything in their natural surroundings was alive with spirits. These

Native American tribes held many ceremonies and festivals.

A medicine man, called a shaman, attends a sick man.

spirits were believed to govern the actions of all animals, plants, water, earth and sky, and weather systems. The Miami prayed to the spirits and made offerings to them.

The Miami were deeply spiritual people, and religious ceremonies were an important part of their life. The tribes held many ceremonies and festivals throughout the year. These celebrations included singing, dancing, and drumming. Together the tribe celebrated good harvests, successful hunts, and victory in battle. There were ceremonies for curing illness, blessing newborn babies, and when children reached adulthood.

The Tribal Council

The spiritual life of the tribe was guided by one of the tribal leaders, a special chief of ceremonies. He was the shaman, or medicine man, who passed along the history of the tribe by telling ancient stories. He was also a healer and spiritual leader in charge of religious ceremonies.

The chief of ceremonies was only one of the two or three chiefs in a tribe. The tribes also had peace chiefs and war chiefs. The position of peace chief was usually passed from father to son. These men traded with other tribes and also resolved difficulties between tribes. The war chief was chosen for his military ability in times of war.

The chiefs kept political and religious unity among the tribes. All important issues were discussed in tribal councils, where the people of the tribe solved problems together. When the tribal councils met, a sacred pipe was shared by those who had come to an agreement. For instance, a peace treaty would be finalized by the ceremony of sharing a sacred pipe filled with tobacco and herbs.

The sacred pipe used in councils was one of the tribe's most valued objects, and it was crafted with

The tribal council shared a sacred pipe.

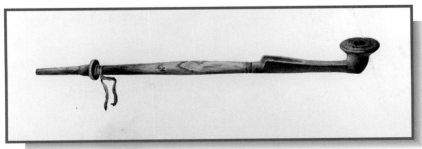

great care. The bowl of the sacred pipe was carved from white, gray, or red pipestone found in the area. The long pipe stem was made from a reed or light wood, often carved with intricate designs. Peace pipes were decorated with white feathers, and pipes used in war councils were decorated with red feathers. Men smoked *kinnikinnik* in sacred pipes. This was made from tobacco and a mixture of dried plant matter including white willow bark.

Disrupted Lives

The lives of the Miami began to change dramatically when the European explorers arrived in 1679. In the 1700s many Miami died from smallpox and other dis-

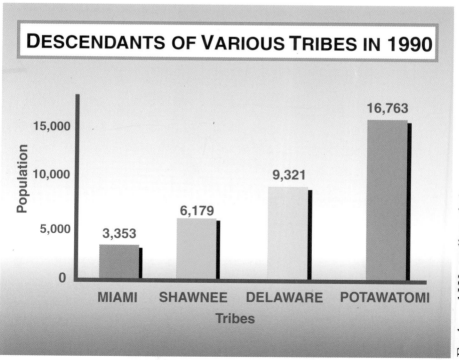

DESCENDANTS OF VARIOUS TRIBES IN 1990

Funk and Wagnalls website.

eases brought by the Europeans. When the Miami chiefs were unable to cure these epidemics, they lost their power as leaders in the community. Confusion, disease, and war increased as tribes from the Northeast were pushed into the area by pioneers moving west.

For a time, the Miami and other natives in the region tried to hold on to their traditional way of life. This became very difficult as European explorers and soldiers came to the area and "Indian Land" was claimed by white people.

Chapter Two

The Fur Traders

The first known European explorer to reach Indiana was a Frenchman, René-Robert Cavelier de La Salle. In 1679 La Salle led a party of twenty-nine explorers from Canada down to the St. Joseph River in Indiana. Like other French explorers who would follow him, La Salle lived in the wilderness with the natives and learned their languages. La Salle stayed only a short while, but he was so impressed with the beauty and fertility of Indiana, he wrote to tell the king of France that the quality of its lands surpassed all others.

The Fur Trade

A year after first visiting Indiana, La Salle returned there as an agent for the French government. The explorer signed a treaty with the Miami that gave parts of Indiana to the French, who called the region New France.

The French had been in North America since the seventeenth century, when they began trading furs with the Native Americans in the Great Lakes region. Fur trapping was incredibly profitable, with the furs of deer, otter, bear, marmot, fox, and beaver selling in Europe for two hundred times what they cost in North America. As a result, the lands claimed by New France were also coveted by the English. By the middle of the seventeenth century, the French and English were battling constantly over who would rule the fur trade in North America.

While these European countries fought over lands inhabited by Native Americans, some tribes aligned themselves with the French. Others sided with the English. The French enlisted the Miami to help them fight against the Iroquois, who owned guns given to

An American trapper sets his beaver traps. The fur trappers sold what they caught for a high profit.

them by the English. The Iroquois were a powerful tribe who prevented the French from exploring the land below the Great Lakes, though France claimed it as its **territory**. The Miami fought fiercely against the Iroquois, though they were outnumbered and had no guns. These battles resulted in many Miami casualties but helped the French gain access to the territory.

Trading Posts and Forts

In 1717 the French set up the first trading post in the Indiana area, Fort Ouiatenon, near present-day Lafayette. The French stocked this post with blankets, cloth, beads, steel knives, brass bells, iron kettles, liquor, and other European items. Tribes who lived in the region traded for these goods with furs from beaver, otter, deer, and muskrat.

Native American tribes traded their furs for European goods.

During this time the French tried to convince the Miami tribe to move north to Detroit, Michigan, where they had a major trading post. The French thought that being closer to their Miami trading partners would give them more control over the fur trade.

When the Miami refused to move, the French sent Captain Charles-Renaud du Buisson in 1721 to build a second post, Fort Miamis, near present-day Fort Wayne and closer to the Miami fur traders. They built a third Indiana outpost, Fort Vincennes, on the Wabash River in 1732.

The French Traders

The French traders lived inside the forts, in houses made from wooden poles with dirt floors and no windows. Outside the fort there was a common garden where the traders planted small plots of vegetables. They added to their meager diets by hunting game. Most of the food, however, arrived with French traders, who traveled to the region in canoes from Canada or New Orleans twice a year. These explorers from the North and South traded food and goods for furs.

Because most of the work trapping fur was done during spring, the traders had a lot of free time. They danced, drank wine, played billiards, staged fistfights and cockfights, and raced horses. They dressed like their Native American neighbors, in leather shirts, leggings, and moccasins. In cold weather they wrapped themselves in buffalo robes. They also mixed with their Native American neighbors—especially the women.

The Catholic priests became so concerned about the behavior of the traders that the French church sent missionaries to take charge of their religious lives and to convert the natives to Catholicism.

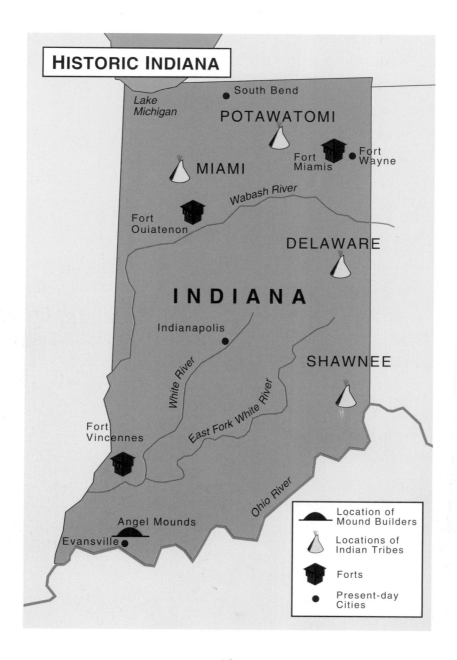

The English Traders

The French authorities also tightened their controls on the fur trade. French traders were required to buy all their goods from the government, which kept prices high. This made it possible for English traders to pay twice the French price for furs. There was a strong temptation among the Native Americans to **bootleg** furs to the English, though they had made agreements with the French.

This helped the English in their efforts to take control of the region. In 1756 England declared war on France, and many battles were fought between the countries in Europe. In America the fighting between

A battle scene from the French and Indian War.

these two powerful countries was called the French and Indian War. Most of the battles in America took place on the East Coast. In Indiana many Native Americans helped the English because they had sold them guns and gave them better prices for their furs. The Miami, however, helped the French, who had peacefully lived among them. The English eventually won the war, taking control of Fort Miamis in 1760, Fort Ouiatenon in 1761, and Vincennes in 1763.

In order to win the trust of the Native Americans, the English king ordered that the lands of Indiana be preserved as Native American hunting grounds. English traders came to the region, but often cheated the Native Americans and refused to give them annual gifts as the French had done. As a result, the Native Americans faced starvation that winter.

Pontiac's War

In 1762 the Ottawa chief Pontiac gathered many tribes together to fight the English. Warriors from the Miami, Potawatomi, Ojibwa, Seneca, and other tribes spent one year making battle plans for what would be known as Pontiac's War.

In 1763 Native American warriors killed or captured soldiers in nine of the eleven English forts north of Indiana along the Great Lakes. They circled the other two forts and starved the men inside.

Native warriors conquered Fort Ouiatenon and destroyed Fort Miamis. The English finally called a peace council in the summer of 1764. They gave the Native

Chief Pontiac united many tribes and urged them to take up the war hatchet against the English.

Americans gifts and promised that Europeans would come there only to trade. No settlers would be allowed to move into the region. New laws created strict penalties for any colonist who settled on Indian land.

This agreement gave hope to the Native Americans, who still thought of the lands of Indiana as their own.

Chapter Three

Battlegrounds

By the time the first shots of the American Revolution were fired in the East Coast colony of Massachusetts in April 1775, Indiana was home to a few thousand white settlers. The population was young, with 80 percent of the men under twenty-one and 95 percent under forty-five. A majority of the settlers were children under ten who were members of large families.

The settlers had a hard life; few people lived to old age. Most homes consisted of a single room, surrounded by three log walls covered with brush. They lacked running water, fireplaces, and other comforts. On freezing winter evenings, the settlers warmed themselves by fire. Life was especially hard on women, who were so worn down by hard work and childbirth that they were easy prey for disease. Many babies died, and the few doctors in the region traveled on horseback with only a few crude medical supplies.

When the war for American independence reached Indiana in 1777, it brought even more hardship for the settlers. The Miami sided with the English after receiving large amounts of food, knives, guns, and other supplies. With help and encouragement from the English, the Miami waged war on the settlers. Women and children were not spared from the terrible bloodshed.

The Northwest Territory

By the time the war ended in 1783, Native Americans still controlled vast areas of the Indiana wilderness. At the same time, the young United States claimed

White settlers lived in one-room log cabins.

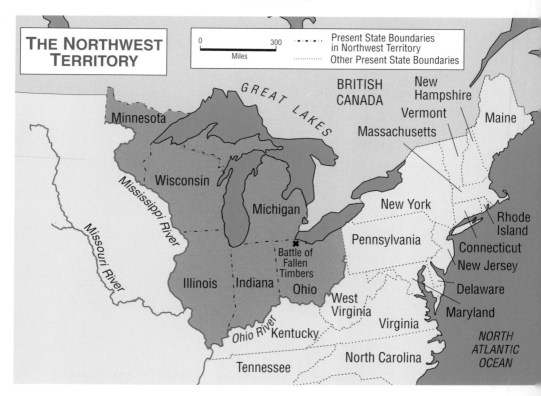

THE NORTHWEST TERRITORY

0 300 Miles

- - - Present State Boundaries in Northwest Territory
.... Other Present State Boundaries

GREAT LAKES

BRITISH CANADA

New Hampshire

Vermont

Maine

Minnesota

Massachusetts

Mississippi River

Wisconsin

Michigan

New York

Rhode Island

Missouri River

Pennsylvania

Connecticut

New Jersey

✖ Battle of Fallen Timbers

Illinois

Indiana

Ohio

West Virginia

Delaware

Maryland

Ohio River

Kentucky

Virginia

NORTH ATLANTIC OCEAN

Tennessee

North Carolina

Indiana as its own. It was part of a region called the Northwest Territory that also included the present-day states of Ohio, Illinois, Michigan, Wisconsin, and part of Minnesota.

In July 1787 **Congress** passed the Northwest Ordinance, which said the Northwest Territory would gradually be divided into three to five states. In the meantime, the territory would be governed by a governor, a secretary, and three judges. When the territory had five thousand white American adult male landowners, it could elect its own lawmakers. When an area had sixty thousand white people living within it, it could apply for statehood.

Little Turtle Fights Back

The rules made by Congress in far-off Pennsylvania did not take Native American desires into account. The Miami and other tribes continued to resist the American invasion of their lands. Miami war chief Little Turtle organized raids on settlements of American pioneers in the 1780s, spreading panic and terror throughout Indiana and beyond. The natives, however, were overpowered by well-armed American soldiers.

In battle after battle, Little Turtle's warriors were beaten until they had all retreated to the town known as Kekionga, near Fort Wayne. By 1790 over a thousand warriors and their families calling themselves the United Tribes of Indiana had gathered in the region. Little Turtle became the general chief of all the warriors, who were from the Miami, Potawatomi, Ottawa, Delaware, Chippewa, Shawnee, and Illinois tribes.

By 1790 the American government decided it must destroy Kekionga to end attacks on American settlers. General Josiah Harmar, commander of the American army, led troops to Kekionga, but native scouts had warned of his approach and the tribes had mysteriously disappeared. The troops attacked Kekionga and other Native American towns along the Maumee River and burned their crops. But the Native Americans were waiting and hiding in the area. Chief Little Turtle led surprise attacks on Harmar's troops and chased them out of Indiana.

Native Americans continued their attacks on American settlements. Meanwhile, the American soldier

Indians prepare to attack settlers. The American government was determined to end this practice.

Arthur St. Clair had become the first governor of the Northwest Territory. In 1791 Congress sent St. Clair to defeat the natives in Kekionga. He formed an army of almost fifteen hundred men for the task.

In 1792 St. Clair's men were surprised in an early morning attack by fewer than 1,000 of Little Turtle's warriors. Over 1,100 white soldiers were killed or wounded and fewer than 66 natives died. This was the worst defeat Americans had ever suffered in any battle with Native Americans.

Because of Little Turtle's victories, Congress talked about making the Ohio River the western boundary of the United States, and leaving Ohio, Indiana, and the lands west for the Native Americans as the English had done. But President George Washington wished to continue the expansion of the nation. He called in General Anthony Wayne, and Congress authorized five thousand troops for him to command.

General Anthony Wayne

In the fall of 1793, General Wayne and his troops established Fort Greenville in southern Indiana. Next

Arthur St. Clair became the first governor of the Northwest Territory.

he established Fort Recovery at the site of Little Turtle's victory over St. Clair. Little Turtle knew that Wayne had a larger, better-armed, and more well-trained army than he had ever faced. Despite this, Little Turtle was persuaded by the other tribal chiefs in June 1794 to attack Wayne's forces. When the natives were defeated, Little Turtle refused to lead any more attacks against General Wayne, because he wanted to

Chief Little Turtle, a great warrior and leader.

save the lives of his people. Warriors who still wanted to fight elected a new leader named Blue Jacket.

On August 15, Wayne and his troops moved toward Kekionga. The Native Americans waited to surprise Wayne at Fallen Timbers. The place, near present-day Toledo, Ohio, was named for the trees that had been scattered about by a tornado. They afforded the Native Americans excellent places to hide while awaiting the arrival of Wayne's troops.

General Wayne had foreseen the danger of the fallen trees to his horsemen. When he realized the Native Americans were waiting in ambush, he sent his soldiers around the trees to attack from the rear. Wayne's men fought a bloody battle against Blue Jacket's warriors with rifles and bayonets in the dense forest.

Betrayal

Realizing that they were outnumbered, the Native warriors fled to a nearby English fort. The English, however, betrayed them—they would not let the warriors in where they had always been welcome before. The English did not want to engage in a fight with Wayne and his soldiers.

After the defeat of the warriors, Wayne and his troops went on to Kekionga, destroying English and Native American property along the way. He burned Kekionga to the ground and established Fort Wayne beside its ruins.

As a result of their defeat at Fallen Timbers, Native Americans gathered at Fort Greenville in the summer of 1795 for a council with General Wayne. The ceremony included long speeches, exchange of wampum (shell beads used as money), gift giving, smoking of peace pipes, and the serving of liquor, carefully timed to insure the best advantage in making a treaty. In exchange for giving up their lands, Native Americans were promised other lands farther west—lands they would have to fight for later on. Little Turtle and the other chiefs signed a treaty opening a large triangular strip of Indiana and half of Ohio to American settlers.

General Anthony Wayne led the American troops to victory over the tribes led by Blue Jacket at the Battle of Fallen Timbers.

A painting depicts the signing of the historic Treaty of Greenville.

The Treaty of Greenville greatly weakened the possibility of a strong, united Native American resistance to American forces. Thousands of settlers began to move into the rich Indiana country north of the Ohio River. But not all Native Americans gave up the defense of their homeland. Raids and even all-out war on American settlers remained a threat until 1815.

Chapter Four

Indiana Statehood

Several factors prevented Indiana from becoming a state right away. The region did not have a large enough white population to qualify for statehood, and the land still officially belonged to the Native Americans. White settlers began moving toward statehood soon after the Treaty of Greenville was signed, however.

As they advanced toward statehood, white settlers gained more local control over their government. White settlers in the region were still being governed by politicians on the East Coast. Many of the laws were not democratic, such as those governing land sales that were structured to favor wealthy eastern developers. Governor St. Clair and his appointed officials were unpopular because they treated the pioneers as inferiors. And only those with large parcels of land were allowed to vote. The growing population of white settlers called for more democracy, finally forcing Governor St. Clair to advance

Shawnee warrior Tecumseh and his twin brother, the Prophet, spoke out for those who did not want to give up their land. Tecumseh had been a young warrior when he fought with Blue Jacket at Fallen Timbers. He was forced to move west from Ohio to Indiana by the Treaty of Greenville, which Little Turtle signed after that defeat. Tecumseh felt that Little Turtle had betrayed his people by giving up their land.

The Battle of Tippecanoe

Under Tecumseh, the tribes of the West from Canada to the Gulf of Mexico came together as the United

Shawnee warrior Tecumseh spoke for the members of tribes who wanted to keep their land.

Tribes of America. Tecumseh felt that a unified nation of tribes might be powerful enough to hold on to some of the Native American land. In the summer of 1810 and again in 1811, Tecumseh and Harrison met at Vincennes to discuss the establishment of a Native American homeland.

Harrison and Tecumseh failed to reach an agreement. Harrison believed that Tecumseh's twin brother, Tenskwatawa—called the Prophet by the whites—was

The Battle of Tippecanoe was a crushing defeat for the Native Americans.

Tenskwatawa, known as the Prophet, was Tecumseh's twin brother.

influencing Tecumseh against making an agreement. The Prophet was a medicine man who preached a return to the traditional tribal ways. To create a center for his movement, he founded Prophet's Town, where the Wabash and Tippecanoe Rivers meet.

On November 7, 1811, while Tecumseh was away persuading tribes in the South to join his union,

Harrison and a thousand troops marched into Prophet's Town and burned it to the ground. The Prophet and most of the four hundred Shawnee warriors escaped. But Harrison's intentions were clear—there would be no more negotiations with the tribes. Tecumseh's movement to unite the tribes of the West was crushed in Indiana on that day.

Tecumseh's final effort at regaining his people's lost land died with him in 1813, during the War of 1812. Tecumseh had joined the British army in its war against America, hoping that a British victory would help him obtain that land. When the war ended in 1815 with an American victory, American settlement

Chief Tecumseh is shot in the chest during battle.

of the Northwest Territory—and statehood for Indiana—was all but assured.

Indiana Becomes a State

By war's end, the gates to the crossroads of America had opened. Thomas Posey had been named as the new governor of the Indiana Territory, and the territorial capital had been moved from Vincennes to the more central settlement at Corydon. Settlers poured into the area on foot, on horseback, in wagons, canoes, and flatboats. Indiana experienced a great increase in population. The Territorial **Assembly** persuaded Congress to begin the legal process of making Indiana a state. Delegates met in Corydon in June 1816, where they **drafted** and approved a **constitution**.

Indiana's constitution was patterned after the constitutions of Kentucky and Ohio. It gave more power to the legislature (lawmakers) and less to the governor and the court system. The constitution made a promise to create a system of public schools and state universities as soon as possible. To do so, it authorized counties to finance public education with money from fines paid by lawbreakers.

The Indiana constitution provided for an election every twelve years to decide whether to change the constitution or write a new one. It also made slavery illegal in the new state, but it did not free those who were already slaves there. Many important citizens, including William Henry Harrison, owned slaves. The population of slaves in Indiana was quite large. Free

A wagon-train camp enjoys a break from the trail. Thousands of settlers like these made the journey to Indiana.

white adult males were given the vote. They were also required, when between the ages of eighteen and forty-five, to serve in the military.

On August 5, 1816, the first Indiana state officials were elected. Jonathan Jennings replaced Thomas Posey as governor. The new U.S. senators were James Noble and Waller Taylor. A newspaperman, William Hendricks, was elected representative to the U.S. Congress. Indiana became a state on December 11, 1816.

By 1820 there were 147,178 settlers clearing the land along the rivers and building settlements in the state of Indiana. That year lawmakers at Corydon decided to move the capital to the site of Fall Creek. In 1821 the General Assembly approved the new location and named it Indianapolis. In the next decade, steam-boats crowded the rivers and the construction of roads began. Indiana was well on its way to becoming the crossroads of America.

Facts About Indiana

State capital and largest city: Indianapolis

State motto: "The Crossroads of America"

State flower: peony

State bird: cardinal

State nickname: Hoosier State

Famous Hoosiers: actor James Dean, President Benjamin Harrison, labor leader Jimmy Hoffa, entertainer David Letterman, composer Cole Porter, and author Kurt Vonnegut Jr.

Natural resources: coal, clay, limestone, natural gas, oil, and timber

Plants raised for food: apples, popcorn, corn, oats, wheat, rye, soybeans, tomatoes, and tobacco

Animal products: turkeys, chickens, eggs, dairy products, cattle, and hogs

Natural plants: aster, iris, orchid, peony, pussy willow, sunflower, and violet

Native birds and animals: bald eagle, beaver, bluebird, cardinal, duck, fox, grouse, horned owl, opossum, peregrine falcon, quail, rabbit, raccoon, robin, skunk, squirrel, weasel, wild turkey, and white-tailed deer

Glossary

allies: People, states, or nations who help each other, especially those who are on the same side in war.

assembly: A group of persons gathered together for a common reason, as for legislative purposes. Also the lower house of the legislature in certain U.S. states.

bootleg: To sell illegally.

Congress: The legislative (lawmaking) branch of the U.S. government, including the Senate and the House of Representatives.

constitution: The system of fundamental laws and principles that prescribes the functions and limits of a government.

delegate: An elected or appointed representative of a U.S. territory in the House of Representatives who is entitled to speak but not vote.

draft: A first outline of a written document to be finished later.

representative: A member of a governmental body, usually legislative, chosen by popular vote, or a member of the U.S. House of Representatives or of the lower house of a state legislature.

stampede: To frighten and cause to suddenly run away in panic; especially a herd of animals that moves together.

territory: A subdivision of the United States that is not a state and is administered by an appointed or elected governor and elected legislature.

For Further Exploration

Books

Marlene Targ Brill, *Celebrate the States: Indiana.* New York: Marshall Cavendish, 1997. Discusses the history of Indiana, as well as its present, its people, and its places of interest.

Ann Heinrichs, *Indiana.* New York: Grolier, 2000. Describes the geography, plants, animals, history, economy, language, religions, culture, sports, arts, and people of the state of Indiana.

Stuart A. Kallen, *Native Americans of the Great Lakes.* San Diego: Lucent Books, 2000. A wide-ranging book about the traditional community life, religious beliefs, and warfare of the native tribes of the Great Lakes region.

Carl Waldman, *Encyclopedia of Native American Tribes.* New York: Facts On File, 1988. A book that explores the history and culture of over 150 Native American tribes.

Website

The official website for the state of Indiana is www.state.in.us.

Index

Picture Credits

About the Authors

Authors Stuart A. Kallen and P. M. Boekhoff live in San Diego, California. Kallen has written more than 150 nonfiction books for children and young adults. He has also written award-winning children's videos and television scripts. Boekhoff is a professional artist. She has cocreated several children's books on the subjects of art and ecology and has illustrated many books covers.